S0-CCK-600

To Bill & Judy,

From Bruce & Gene

We love being in your
book study group & in the same
congregation with you. Hope you
enjoy this beautiful book of
Maple Ridge -

B & G -

Maple Ridge

Moments in Time

. . . .

BY MARILYN TIMMS

M stands for maple trees

A stand for Alouette River

P stands for lots of nice people

L stands for a place to learn

E stands for many events

R stands for it does not matter what race you are

I stands for ice cream trucks on sunny days

D stands for the many dykes in our area

G stands for Golden Ears Park

E stands for enjoy Maple Ridge

Sarah V Neal, 10

Maple Ridge

Moments in Time

Celebrating 125 years

WRITTEN BY
CHRIS CAMPBELL, LYNN EASTON AND ALAN WOODLAND

FOREWORD BY SHEILA NICKOLS

EDITED BY LYNN EASTON

PHOTOGRAPHY BY BOB HERGER

THE DISTRICT OF MAPLE RIDGE

PRODUCED BY BOB HERGER IN ASSOCIATION WITH
THE DISTRICT OF MAPLE RIDGE,
RIDGE MEADOWS ARTS COUNCIL
AND THE MAPLE RIDGE HISTORICAL SOCIETY

FIRST EDITION 1999

Text and Photography Copyright © 1999

All right reserved. No part of this publication may be reproduced or transmitted in any form or by any means, electronic or mechanical, including photocopying, recording, or by any information storage and retrieval system, now known or to be invented, without permission in writing from the publisher.

Published by Bob Herger

Written by Chris Campbell, Lynn Easton & Alan Woodland

Photography by Bob Herger

Design by Kelly Brooks

Printed in Singapore

CANADIAN CATALOGUING IN PUBLICATION DATA

ISBN 0-9685335-0-7

This book may be ordered from
Bob Herger (604) 463-9482

Contents

Foreword BY SHEILA NICKOLS

This year we are celebrating one moment in time for our beautiful part of the world. On September 12, 1874 the scattering of new settlers in this land gathered to form a brand new municipal government, calling it Maple Ridge.

While we honour those families that came here, drawn by the challenge of turning almost untouched forest and wild places into farmland and villages, we remember that they were not the first people to inhabit this area. First Nations people lived here for uncounted years, after the land lifted free from the last ice age and waters flowed in something close to the present banks. The natural boundaries were the same as today – what we call the Fraser River to the south; the incomparable sweep of mountains to the north; the Stave River to the east; and on the west, the Pitt River. These rivers and waterways threading our land like arteries were the travelling routes for people skilled in turning the abundant and easily – worked cedar trees into canoes.

The Katzie people were not driven from their winter habitation in cedar longhouses by the Hammond brothers looking to establish a town, or even by the earlier raids of the Kwakutl from the north of Vancouver Island. Settlers arriving here in the 1860s saw empty dwellings deserted because of the lethal smallpox epidemic that raged through the coastal area in the late 1700s. Surviving members of the Pierre family preserved in memory many legends from the Katzie lore, like the tale of Swaneset, creator of the Alouette River and the sloughs of Pitt Meadows. Their stories also tell how ancestors used the peaks of the Golden Ears to anchor a canoe during the time of a great flood.

Today, if you ask anyone in Maple Ridge what are the heritage features that should be preserved, high on the list are all our natural treasures. We must save the clean flowing rivers and streams that nature has given us, as well as the trees and wild spaces remaining in many parts of our municipality. We would like our great-grandchildren to know and respect the landscape we hand down. Some well preserved heritage buildings make the list, like St. John the Divine Anglican Church and Haney House, and some of the magnificent maple trees that gave our community name and identity, like the two standing sentinel at the north end of Maple Ridge Cemetery.

Something equally valuable that can't be seen or photographed is our amazing community spirit. Perhaps it was the need to work together in the early days that fostered a tradition of self-help and sharing that led to such firmly based institutions as the annual fair, held almost every year since 1901 and still a showcase for young farmers and community groups. Our festivals, parades and public celebrations are a cherished part of our living heritage. Volunteers have fought fires, built community halls, founded churches and service groups, and insisted that we needed and deserved a library, a hospital, a community hall and a museum.

Pioneer families, with their own legends and stories, know the history of Maple Ridge because they helped create it. Newcomers sense that there is more here than a good place to live, and often go on to become our most active and giving volunteers. In the celebration of our 125 years as a municipality, let us remember where we came from, who we are now, and what we aspire to become.

This book project is a striking tribute to the enthusiasm of those newcomers and the efforts of all who have made this community home since those early days. Well-respected Maple Ridge photographer Bob Herger has brought together local writers, painters, and school children to share their visions of our community – past and present.

This colourful montage of words and pictures comes together in a poetic and engaging manner which teaches us a little about our shared history while celebrating the people of Maple Ridge and the land which surrounds us.

RIDGE OF MAPLES

Yellow fire
still hot in the Autumn sun
falls unforgotten in the blaze of new ideas.
Named and pressed between wax paper,
wrapped to keep the memory of heat
until the thaw of spring.

An axe would bring the sounds
of violins and keep the walls from winter wind.
But stubborn veins of dying leaves defy,
shout life in bursts of burnt magenta
Prepare for cold with bold abandon,
a blanket at the feet.

LYNN EASTON

Maple Ridge was named in 1874 for a stand of Big Leaf Maples (acer Macrophyllum) which overlooked
the Fraser River for three kilometres from Hammond to Haney. The town adopted the title
from settler John McIver's dairy farm 'Maple Ridge', which was located on what is now the
Maple Ridge Golf Course, and once included that impressive ridge of knotted Maples.

PORT HANEY B.C.

. . . .

A young Hugh Morse poses with proud store
clerks on Ontario St. (now 224th
looking south to the Fraser River)
during the mid-1920s when this street was
the hub of local commerce.

PHOTO COURTESY OF MAPLE RIDGE MUSEUM

Past, Present & Perhaps

BY ALAN WOODLAND

*T*he Municipality of Maple Ridge lies folded into gently rising land between the mountains now known as the Golden Ears and the great winding river named for explorer and adventurer, Simon Fraser.

It would not be too fanciful to call it a jewel in the necklace of the Fraser, a pearl situated in surroundings of such beauty that a resident could travel ten thousand miles by plane and train and bus, camel or mule or yak, and on arrival, find no greater beauty than at the beginning of the journey.

Away from home, what do we tell the stranger about our town and why we have chosen to live here? Is it the natural setting, with ease of access to places that have not yet been tamed? Is it the sense of belonging that still exists, even though the community is growing rapidly? Is it the existence of areas within Maple Ridge, each with its own personality, where residents can find their own individual environment?

Out of the country, when asked where we live, we probably say 'British Columbia'. In Ontario or Manitoba, the same question will be answered with something like, 'Oh, up the Fraser Valley 40-kilometres east of Vancouver.' But closer to home we say we live in Albion or Hammond, Haney or Ruskin, Webster's Corners, Whonnock or Yennadon: unique communities that give Maple Ridge its special character.

The history of Maple Ridge is written in the names on gravestones and on the cenotaph; names of pioneers and volunteers, and of the athletes and scholars who make us proud to share in their successes; names of the original seven councillors elected on October 3, 1874 and all who have succeeded them; names of people who were born here and those who came here from all over the world; names of the streets, fields and hills, parks and corners and of those seven close-knit communities that are the vital parts of the municipality.

The history of Maple Ridge can be found in its stores, markets, gas stations, cafes and barbershops; in the curling rink and fire halls, the sawmills and shake mills along the river, and the fish boats tied up at the wharves, waiting for an opening.

Its history is under glass in the greenhouses, in the silos and the cattle barns, in fruit storage sheds, wayside vegetable stands and in stables from one end of the municipality to the other. Its history is in the churches and the schools, and, fortunately for us living now, it is recorded in the minutes of clubs and societies, in old newspapers and photographs, and a few books.

There are stories of arrival and departure, of settling in and becoming part of neighbourhood and community; happy stories, funny stories, sad stories of births, graduations, marriages and deaths; great summers and unusual winters, of fire and flood and fever. Stories that are part of the heart that beats beneath the surface of the Maple Ridge of today. A community of communities unique in its citizens and in the chronology of its events.

We have heard the stories of the arrival of the first Hudson's Bay Company party in 1824 and the establishment, three years later, of a fortified trading post across the river at what is now Fort Langley.

For many of us this is the first we are told of the local native peoples who lived along the river. They fished the salmon and gathered wild fruits and vegetables and traded them, along with furs, for manufactured goods from the Hudson's Bay Company.

The earliest white settlers in Maple Ridge had been employees of the Hudson's Bay Company. Samuel Robertson, a carpenter and boat builder, planted an orchard east of Kanaka Creek and in 1858, pre-empted the lowland which is now Albion.

In 1859, John McIver, a cooper, began clearing the heavily timbered land where Maple Ridge golf course is today. He named the dairy farm he established there, 'Maple Ridge' after the 'ridge of beautiful maple trees which stretched for two miles along the river, from what is now Hammond to Slide Hill in Haney.' It was this name that was chosen in 1874 to be the name of the new municipality.

We have heard the story of the 165 handpicked Royal Engineers who laid out the capital at New Westminster, surveyed and mapped the country, designed the first schools and churches, directed the sale of land and kept order among the gold seekers – all within five short years. When the Royal Engineers were disbanded in 1863, John McKenney and his brother-in-law, James Lindsay, took up land close to John McIver. Louis Bonson settled in what was to become Hammond.

During the next twenty years those early arrivals were joined by settlers whose names are as much a part of the history of Maple Ridge as are the maples themselves: William Howison, Henry Dawson, William Nelson, who built a wharf for passing paddlewheelers; the other Robertson, Robert, also a Hudson's Bay man, the first white settler in Whonnock; John and William Hammond, who in 1872, pre-empted 120 acres and founded the town of Hammond; John Bell, W.H. Newton, James Thorne, Peter Baker, James Best, whose home served for a while as the Presbyterian church; and Thomas Haney who gave his name to the townsite of Port Haney when it was formally registered in 1882.

In pioneer times it is usually only the names of the men that are listed as land owners, founders and builders. The names of the women are harder to find. In Maple Ridge: a History of Settlement, a valuable source for knowing our history, there is a moving tribute to the community's pioneer women by Mrs. Alex Stevenson, who arrived in Port Haney in 1892, when the tiny community had 'next to no gravel on the roads' and 'neither butcher nor baker, nor barber'. She talks of the hardships they faced and the strength of character and resilience they showed.

Her words take us back to the early years when there was no electricity; no switches to bring light and heat, sound and pictures; no motors humming to provide cool and comfort; no telephone or internet.

If early residents wanted music, they made it themselves; played it on an old fiddle, an accordion, or a rare piano that had been brought up the bank from the river on the backs of willing helpers. If they wanted to talk with friends living a mile or two across town, they harnessed up the horse and buggy or walked the rough trails.

Women worked with men to clear the land, tend the farm, raise the children and create a sense of community. Churches and meeting halls were built, schools were opened, teachers hired, post offices, stores and businesses were established and residents came together to celebrate and to bury their dead. After a time, individuals were selected to govern and help solve the problems of the day. There were good times and bad.

Past and present. It is morning now. As the sun rises over the mountains, walk past the mill at Hammond, the fresh smell of cedar in the air. Cross the invisible boundary into Haney and after a while stand outside historic St. John the Divine Church. It was built by Royal Engineers in 1859 at Derby on the south side of the Fraser, dismantled in 1882, floated across the river and rebuilt close to its present site near the corner of Laity Street. Think about that. Then as you walk east along the old River Road, once the main artery in and out, imagine an earlier time with hand-made wagon wheels mumbling over corduroy and hear the horses snorting in the dust.

Down by Port Haney Wharf, imagine the early residents arriving for work, ordinary men and women keeping the little town alive, giving it shape and purpose, doing business to the swish and rustle of long dresses, the clip of boots on the boardwalk. They call to each other. A steamboat sounds its whistle.

Walk across the CPR tracks and onto the wharf. Look east and west up and down the river. Imagine. In the beginning the only road was the river, flowing wide and brown through our history.

The Fraser River – overflowing in summer, frozen in winter. Friend and enemy and only avenue to the logging camps and the lumber mills, gold mines, orchards and berry farms; silver hoard for the fisherman; highway for the farmer who sailed or rowed his harvest down to New Westminster's market and came back with essential tools and equipment.

Pause at the foot of 224th Street, once called 8th Avenue and before that, Ontario Street. Walk up the hill, passing Thomas Haney's fine house, now linked to the wharf and the Maple Ridge Museum by the Heritage River Walk. Cross the Lougheed Highway and walk towards the mountains, passing the civic gardens and the bandstand where listeners gather on the lawn on summer nights, music floats among the trees, the sun sets and the early stars come out. Stop at the cenotaph and read the names of the men who lived and played and worked here; who left the safety and serenity of their family homes and farms and ventured into foreign lands to fight for something they believed in – and did not come back.

Walk up to the Dewdney Trunk Road, the other main link between Maple Ridge and the Valley, and you will find 224th Street doesn't go straight north and south. There is a jink at the intersection because a big tree grew there and, for a long time, nobody wanted to cut it down. It has gone now, sadly, along with many of the fine, old trees as the community grows steadily east and west and towards the mountains.

Past and present. Some idea of early life in Maple Ridge can be had from articles in newspapers in 1910, 1911, and 1912. The first from the Fraser Valley Record, reports that the March 1910, monthly meeting of the Maple Ridge council was held in Whonnock. It was the custom of council to meet in the eastern part of the district once in each year.

The Record tells us that 'the party arrived from Haney by the ten o'clock train and proceeded to inspect the proposed new road over Whonnock Creek'. It was eleven o'clock when they reached the schoolhouse. Present day councillors will be delighted to hear that 'the reeve addressed the meeting, stating it was held in Whonnock to give the residents a chance of complaining of any grievance and he was ready to hear any ratepayer who had any suggestion to make or any petition to ask.' There was considerable discussion about the dog tax.

In the British Columbian Weekly of August 15, 1911, there is an upbeat article that reports on the new Bank of Montreal being built on River Road and adds, 'Mr. Martyn is building a barber shop for Mr. Andrew Lytle, who has already taken possession and is cutting hair and giving clean shaves before the doors and windows are in the building.'

The following year, in 1912, shortly before the 38th birthday of Maple Ridge, the Columbian Newspaper published a special Fraser Valley edition with a full page for the municipality and a half page each for Haney and Hammond. There are glowing tributes to Maple Ridge. The newspaper draws attention to the ease with which the locals can ship their abundant and sought-after produce by rail or river, with more than 100 cars of freight shipped monthly from the Port Haney CPR station.

. . . .

In 1921, Mrs. Mary Kershaw tended to her charges
at the U.K. Poultry Farm, located in an area at the end
of 240th Street known as Dingle Dell. Though left out of
many of the history books, women were integral to the
establishment and growth of Maple Ridge.

PHOTO COURTESY OF MAPLE RIDGE MUSEUM

Port Hammond is described as 'a thrifty little shipping point and serious contender for first honours in the municipality.' It remained a close rival to Haney, growing through the 1910s and 1920s at roughly the same pace, competing in business and commerce until road transport, both private and commercial, eclipsed that of rail and river. Hammond's fortunes dwindled when the Lougheed Highway was built through what was to become the centre of Haney, bypassing the mill and rail community to the south. But the shifting of heavy traffic to the north has given modern day Hammond a quiet charm, its residents enjoying a sense of being linked to the past and the heritage around them.

In those quiet months, before the first world war changed their lives forever, the people of Maple Ridge looked towards the future. Present day residents will be pleased to know that according to the Columbian, 'The summer seasons are delightful, humidity being unnoticeable and extreme heat is alien. There is quite a precipitation of rain during three of the winter months but only sufficient to supply plenty of moisture for the growing season.'

Maple Ridge is recommended as an ideal place to play as well as live and farm. Kanaka Creek, the Lillooet (Alouette) River and local lakes 'abound with trout and other finned gamesters while the country surrounding them is a favourite haunt of numberless species of wild game.'

'There has never been any of the "boom" element in Maple Ridge and it is desired by those most deeply interested in its welfare to eliminate any semblance of such, for a steady, profitable growth is more to be desired than spasmodic prosperity.' Words that are echoed today.

Because Maple Ridge is a real place, with real people living real lives, not everything in its garden is lovely. Sometimes it suffers from growing pains and not all of its growth is pleasing to its residents. Sometimes they have to work together in attempting to balance their influence against the influence of those who would change their hometown in ways they find unacceptable.

Past, present, and future. The place we call Maple Ridge is changing and growing daily. To appreciate that growth we can look at the evidence around us: the high-rise apartment blocks, the long awaited hospital, one in a succession of municipal halls, the courthouse, public library, police station, several fire stations, community halls, numerous churches, clusters of condominiums, schools, parks and play grounds, often named after local residents; and businesses that have served several generations: Fuller-Watson Department store (since 1924), Mussallem Motors (since 1919),R. Muth and Sons (since 1945), Bruce's Market (since 1948) and the Bank of Montreal (since l911), all now on the Lougheed Highway; Haney Builders (since 1938); Maple Ridge golf course (since 1925); and the Hammond mill, which under various names and ownerships, dates back to 1910.

But along the way, much that was once familiar to the residents of Maple Ridge has disappeared. The Berryland Cannery on the Dewdney Trunk Road; Haney Brick and Tile and the A & L Lumber Company above the river; the Haney, Hammond and Whonnock CPR stations; hotels and stores on River Road before the Lougheed Highway, completed in l931, brought the town up the hill; and the Agricultural (Aggie) Hall in the centre of Haney.

Although we have had change and upheaval, we've been lucky there have been no great physical catastrophes here. We have had our share of small earthquakes that rattled the china in the kitchen and moved pictures on the walls; and we can still see evidence of the disturbance in 1880 that sent part of Maple Ridge, a quarter of a mile long, sliding down into the Fraser. The slide demolished a section of River Road, effectively separating Haney from Hammond.

Fires, epidemics and floods challenged the residents, brought them together and, sometimes, moved the municipality forward. Communities that relied on wood for construction and fuel were constantly in danger of fire. In 1916, almost the entire business section of Hammond was destroyed. In 1926, a fire started in B.C. Fruit Growers' cold storage plant. It burned most of the nearby buildings on both sides of River Road at the Haney wharf. 1926 saw a fire begin at Gold Creek and rage though what is now Golden Ears Park, almost bringing the successful Abernethy-Lougheed logging operations to a halt. A 1931 fire destroyed the Haney C.P.R. station and the Pacific Grower's store across the street. In 1953, the Maple Ridge High School caught fire and burned to the ground.

During the diphtheria epidemic of 1888-89, homes were quarantined and a temporary hospital was set up. Two children died. Shortly afterwards council established a board of three councillors to oversee the health of the community. Schools were closed and public gatherings cancelled during the Spanish influenza outbreak of 1918-1919 that caused the death of 40,000,000 people around the world and took the lives of several Maple Ridge residents.

The great Fraser flood of 1894 created widespread destruction in low lying areas of the municipality. In 1896, the residents of the lowlands near Pitt River left Maple Ridge to become an unorganized territory, in an attempt to obtain better flood control from the provincial government. The area remained unorganized for eighteen years before being incorporated as the Municipality of Pitt Meadows in 1914.

The flood of 1948 is still very much in the memory of older residents and in the minds of those whose job it is to monitor the level of the river. The coincidence of the numbers 1894 and 1948 led many to believe there would be another flood in 1984. Residents living in the flood plain worried but the runoff was normal and the great river flowed gently past Maple Ridge and down to the delta.

Fires, epidemics and floods, the stuff of history. But history is also made of gentler stuff like a Christmas party held in the new town hall on Callaghan Street in 1893, which drew settlers from miles around. Maple Ridge writer and historian, Edward Villiers, sets the scene:

'Early on Saturday morning a fire was lit in the big wood burning heater in the Haney Hall. Fir boughs were brought in to decorate the walls. Benches were slid against the walls. Babies and small children were whisked upstairs to be bundled in assorted rugs, blankets and coats.'

'Music was provided by two fiddles played alternately by Hector Ferguson and Adam Docksteader, and August and Alonzo Baker. The Bakers had walked in from Albion, crossing Kanaka Creek on the CPR trestle. Around midnight more food was served. The dance lasted until daybreak.'

Children enjoy the freedom of boating on the Alouette River
during a 1940s community picnic at Maple Ridge Park,
now the oldest picnicking spot in the community.

PHOTO COURTESY OF MAPLE RIDGE MUSEUM

A modern-day father and son begin a leisurely
outing as the sun rises on the Alouette River.

"Past, present and perhaps," my father used to say, liking the sound of the three ps and reminding us that the future is not always certain. As the past becomes the present and we move further from those early years, it becomes ever more difficult to understand the daily experiences of the pioneer men, women and children who cut their homes from the bush, built trails, roads and bridges to connect them, cleared the land, planted and harvested their crops, all by hand with simple tools and with only horses and oxen to help them.

To know them, we rely on the few letters and diaries they found time to write, usually at night by oil lamp or candlelight, when the days work was done. We rely on the memories of people who listened carefully to their parents and grandparents and recorded what they said; and of long-time residents like Brian Byrnes of Whonnock, who has shared his stories and made sure that they will not be forgotten.

The Byrnes garage on the Lougheed Highway had a large stove which like a magnet attracted work crews, commercial travellers and men who sought warmth and company on a cold winter's day.

Space permits only limited recognition of the rich diversity of people who built this place; people who came from all parts of the world and brought their skills and labour to the land, industry and commerce of Maple Ridge. There were the British who arrived early, either directly from the British Isles or from eastern Canada and the United States; Kanakas from the Sandwich Islands (Hawaii)who crossed the river to live and work in Albion after labouring for the Hudson's Bay Company at Fort Langley; Chinese labourers who worked on the railway and, when it was completed, stayed to work in the brick works and mills; Norwegians who pioneered and left their mark on Whonnock; Finnish settlers who brought their sense of community to Webster's Corners; the Japanese who mastered the business of fruit cultivation and poultry farming in Haney, Whonnock and Ruskin, their residence here brought to an abrupt halt in 1942 when they were forced to leave the area during World War Two; and later, Dutch, German and Indo Canadian immigrants, each bringing their own special energy and cultural gifts.

From early times the residents of Maple Ridge excelled in a variety of sports. As the community developed and facilities became available, they came together to skate and play hockey (when it was cold enough) and to swim in the lakes and rivers (when it was warm enough). There were clubs for riding, golf and gymnastics, badminton and tennis, softball and baseball, with games played at Fall Fairs. In the 1920s, Hammond and Haney fielded teams in the Dewdney Baseball League and in 1924, the Hammond Cedar team won the B.C. championship with a team stacked with hotshots from across North America, thanks to Doan Hartnell owner of Hammond (then Bailey's) Cedar.

In modern times, teams from Maple Ridge have competed successfully in all manner of sport and individual athletes have brought us international fame. It is fitting that the inaugural ceremony of the local Hall of Fame, during which seven of the community's finest athletes were inducted, should take place in our 125th anniversary year.

*Ruskin Community Hall, built in 1922 and still in
operation, was one of dozens of thriving community
gathering places that sprung up in the early
years of Maple Ridge.*
BY ROBERTA COMBS

23

The names and records of achievements of Ann Meraw (swimming), Marietta Bell, who competed in the '30s and '40s as Rita Panasis (basketball and softball), Debbie Brill (high jump), Tom Dinsley (diving), Cam Neely (hockey), Larry Walker (baseball) and Greg Moore (auto racing) are to be placed in a Hall of Fame planned for the new civic centre.

Maple Ridge can claim a number of honorary titles: Horse Capital of the North Fraser, Gateway to the Golden Ears, Home of the Beast, The Outdoor Jazz and Blues Festival City – but the one that tops them all is Community of Volunteers.

There is no shortage of volunteers for any sporting or cultural events. Volunteers greet you in the Maple Ridge Art Gallery, volunteers bring caring support to patients in the hospital and children in schools; volunteers risk their lives in the mountains and at fires; volunteers are ready to help people with problems, people in trouble, people who are hungry and without a home. Since 1991, the Maple Ridge Community Foundation has selected a volunteer to receive the Citizen of the Year Award and each year the municipality hosts an appreciation day in recognition of the invaluable contribution given willingly and freely by its citizens.

For the past 25 years a group of older men, affectionately known as the Maple Ridge Senate, has met for coffee and conversation at various locations in Haney. In response to a query as to what they felt had been the most important influences and events in the history of the community, they selected the Gazette, which was first printed in Hammond in 1919, moved to Haney in 1926, and, with various owners and editors, recorded the daily life of Maple Ridge until 1985; and the local logging and lumber industry, exemplified by the Abernethy – Lougheed Logging Company, which operated through the 1920s; and the Hammond Mill which began small in 1910 and grew to be the largest red cedar mill in the world.

For the most far-reaching events, the Senate chose the arrival of the C.P.R. in the 1880s, the floods of 1894 and 1948, the building of the Lougheed Highway from 1928 to 1931 and the expulsion of Japanese residents in l942.

Events like these give us points of departure when we are trying to remember. We say, 'Oh yes, that was before the Lougheed was pushed through.' or, 'I remember, because our Japanese friends stopped coming to school that year.' Many long time residents identify an incident in their lives as having been before or after the forty-eight flood.

By the end of this year in which we celebrate the 125th anniversary of the incorporation of the Municipality of Maple Ridge there will have been 125 Christmases, Easters, Hallowe'ens and Thanksgivings. 125 springs, summers, falls and winters. 125 returns to school after summer vacations spent outdoors on the farm or at the beach.

125 years of getting together to raise funds to build the churches, community halls and schools, with basket socials, lantern slides, quilting bees, sing-songs, garden parties, teas, craft fairs, bake sales, cake walks, plays, concerts and dances.

125 years during which the history and personality of Maple Ridge has unfolded day by day, season by season.

125 years of growth from the handful of settlers who were here in 1874 to the more than 60,000 residents living here today.

One of the reasons we mark an anniversary is to remember and celebrate the past that makes the present possible. We all live on the backs of those who came before, benefiting from their labours and far-sighted decisions. We drive their roads and cross their bridges and build houses on land they cleared. It is appropriate that we honour them.

But anniversaries have other functions too. They give us an opportunity to take inventory in the present, to see how far we've come and how we got here; to see what we've achieved and how we intend to proceed into the future. There are questions we should ask. What will future generations have to honour us for? How much of the heritage we enjoy will we pass on intact or enhanced to them? How seriously do we take our stewardship of the precious resources we inherited? Will there be fish in the rivers; fresh fruit from local farms in the markets and stores? Will future residents enjoy safe streets and well-maintained parks for recreation? What aspects of life in Maple Ridge do we wish to pass on to our grandchildren?

This year, in which we are celebrating our 125th anniversary, is passing – just as all the years of our history have passed. It will not be long before 1999 comes to an end and this book will be part of the past, part of the history of a special place between the mountains and the river – a place we are proud to call home.

Maple Ridge *Moments in Time*

In its 125 year history, Maple Ridge has grown,
from a few wooden-framed homes and businesses,
to a community of more than 60,000.
PHOTO BY DON WAITE

*Bill Hampton looks to the future while working land his family has
been farming for 121 years. His property has been named a century farm
and his method reflects old values and traditions in our modern times.*

PEOPLE IN TIME

❧

We have grown from separate pioneer communities rising out of demanding landscapes which determined where we would live: below the mountains, beside the Fraser River, along the streams and creeks.

People built these communities, one by one, with stubborn determination and optimism. Webster's Corners, Ruskin, Hammond, Albion, Yennadon, Thornhill and every neighbourhood in between. Once settled, people gathered around stores, halls, churches, farm fields and playing fields to create our history. They started theatre companies and local businesses. Arts groups and church groups. Pony clubs and poetry clubs. They waged political fights at home and fought wars far away.

Others are barely mentioned in our history books at all. They stare at us from one of thousands of museum photos like old friends – pioneers and newcomers who've made their mark in subtle ways. Bringing new cultures and traditions. Organizing neighbourhood groups. Volunteering to fight fires. Walking the dykes. Tilling backyard gardens. Meeting at beaches and ice rinks. They were – just as we are today – making history.

We are more multicultural. Less agricultural. Different from our history. We've created a future those pioneers could never have imagined, and a past our children will peer at with bewilderment. This is our place in time – the present – in this thriving municipality where we believe community still means working and playing together along the rivers and below the mountains.

The Fall Fair BY LYNN EASTON

It was 1901 and dreams that our new agricultural show might some day rival the size of the Cloverdale fair were in the air. The ferns were cut and swamps filled, labour traded for space by those who wanted courts and fields. By those who could see home in the hills.

But why work so hard? To judge another zucchini. Taste another pie. The records show who has won each year since. Complete with width and breadth of each root vegetable. Praise for this year's bull. Year after year, after year, after year. List after List.

Those 4-H names of a century ago sound a lot like ours. Some are. The Laitys. The Davisons. The old lists sound a lot like our lists of this year's winners at the school bazaar, poetry winners, softball champions. Names. To remind us who we are.

There is no more Aggie Hall in which to call the winners names but we can watch a show of stars and fireworks under the open skies. There are high-tech rides and state-of-the-art sound systems. But the lists remain. Best jelly. Best longhaired goat. Best lamb. 4-H hopefuls hover near the judges station. Their names will be added to the others. The thousands of others who took the time to bake and cook, to shine their sheep, and feed their pigs. Each year, they show us, again, that lists are made of people. People who have carved home out of the hills.

There is one fair that me and my mom and dad
always go to, and one of my favourite things in
it is Sergio the bull. He is really big and flies like
to climb on him. *Rebecca Jamieson, 8*

Peaceful Music BY LYNN EASTON

The names are listed alphabetically. Simply. Without fanfare.

There are, sadly, similar monuments in communities all across this country which dedicate in stone our thanks to a generation taken from our fields and factories to fight a war half a world away.

But this is our cenotaph, they were our men, and now this is our place to remember. And each year on November 11th we do. These dozens of men and all others lost in war are honoured with a quiet ceremony in a small, treed garden on a busy boulevard. Each year, while the memories of those who fought may fade, the crowds in Centennial Peace Park grow larger. A new generation silently saluting the past and promising to remember into the future.

Young children on large shoulders listen to tearful trumpets. They imagine unknown forefathers and sway as they wait for the parade to begin. That is surely what those survivors had in mind when they carved the stone and placed it in Centennial Park for all to see. Children free from the knowledge of war. Free to dance.

And dance they do in Centennial Park. This lush green oasis in the middle of the commercial downtown of Maple Ridge has become a magnet for community gatherings in a community renowned for its gatherings. Mountain Festival ceremonies, Canada Day celebrations, Blues and Jazz Festivals, and Easter egg hunts are all held in the park and centred around a spot known simply as The Bandstand.

The bandstand itself was built in 1994 with copper, steel, stone, and the sweat of countless people including a stubborn World War Two veteran who had the vision to see it built.

The names of those who gave money and time to turn the vision into reality are engraved in brass, a stone's throw away from the cenotaph where the names of lost soldiers are recalled each year.

Today, young hands touch the engravings distractedly as they pass through the shade of the Peace Park. A brief hello as they head for the music. Free to dance.

A young boy brings his trombone to life with a tune. BY CINDI HOFLIN

GHOSTS OF 1942

There are ghosts in this town.

They once lived in orchards and one-room schools, baseball fields, boats, and busy canneries.

Now they float out of long lists and longer memories, whispering to open mouths and minds.

Some fished. Some fought. Most bought

land milled into reputations of superiority

until That Day

When they disappeared from churches, chores,

and half-tilled fields.

Leaving a legacy of land. Acres and acres of land – used – to make this place a town.

. . . .
Crowds gather for Canada Day
ceremonies at the Centennial
Park bandstand.
PHOTO CHUCK RUSSELL

My other favourite thing is when

Canada has its birthday and we get

to play and dance together at the

bandstand. *Rebecca Jamieson, 8*

A young Irish dancer prepares for her
turn in the spotlight.

BY ROBERTA COMBS

Meeting Place *BY CHRIS CAMPBELL*

A father and son saunter up a slight slope toward the concrete and metal bridge at 224th Street and 128th Avenue. It's a hot day, perfect for a cool walk under the trees at the South Alouette River, which acts as nature's own form of air conditioning system.

The boy clutches a long green leaf as the river catches his eye. He's curious. Too short to see over the railing, the boy stands on the bottom rung and stares, watching the water flow westward.

The father speaks softly, gesturing with thick hands towards the trees. Then the river bank. Finally the water. I can't hear what he says over the noise of water hitting rock. Wouldn't want to. This is a private moment between men.

....

Welcome to the world of Maple Ridge's bridges – the ultimate meeting place.

Not big bridges where thousands meet in rush-hour traffic, but the14 municipal bridges managed by the District of Maple Ridge which vary in size and style from solid concrete spans to tiny beat-up wood planks that shake under your feet – if you bounce too hard.

These bridges share a common feature: they are seductive. I know. I've fallen for them. The pull is magnetic. There are few things more tranquil than spending a moment on a bridge looking at water rushing towards you, or washing away. Such moments are often brief, but they are exquisite. Simply plant your elbows down on the railing, dangle your hands over the side and stand for a moment. Search for birds hiding in the trees or fish making their way upstream. Chances are you'll meet someone new.

....

It's a busy time at the South Alouette bridge. A young man, sleek-and-narrow shades slung over the top of his head, stands on the river bank whipping his fishing rod back and forth. He doesn't know it, but he's giving a fascinating flyfishing demonstration.

A young mom pulls a blue plastic wagon towards the bridge with her son in tow. Inside the wagon, the child straddles picnic supplies: chips, pop and a watermelon as big as the boy playing bongos on it. Curious, the boy climbs onto the bottom rung of the bridge, staring at the fishing rod darting back and forth down below. The line barely touches the water with each motion before it gets snagged on the rail of the bridge. The man tugs to no avail. The boy races over to help untie it. As he does, he asks that ultimate kid question. "What're you doing?"

....

Different bridges give different perspectives.

The smallest is the span over Millionaire/Hennipen Creek, which feeds into the South Alouette River. Most drivers heading out to Alouette Lake might miss it. Located at Fern Crescent and 129th Avenue, it takes all of eight paces to cross. From this vantage point the Alouette is shallow. Water barely clears the rocks on this narrow stretch, but stop at the bridge at the north end of 216th Street and you get an entirely different view. The Alouette at this point is deep, wide, and lumbering as numerous tributaries have joined forces before easing into the Pitt River. Bridges provide the best view of these everchanging rivers, creeks and tiny streams. And every time you visit one, you discover something or someone new.

....

All is quiet at the green metal bridge spanning Blaney Creek at the northern end of 224th Street. I think I'm alone until I hear a voice in the wilderness. Two men glide under the bridge and head east until their boat touches bottom and they struggle to turn it around, chatting as they work their paddles. "We just ran out of water," one says. They pass under the bridge ready to head home when one of the paddlers turns and asks, "Where are we anyway?"

You're in Maple Ridge.

. . . .

. . . .

Kanaka Creek is an inviting spot for all types
of recreation, including a little sailing.
BY RON HEDRICK.

I used to be a city
boy, but now I'm a
country hillside boy.
Gary Louis, 10

Red and White and Square

. . . .

BY LYNN EASTON

There's a barn just beyond downtown Maple Ridge.

It's red and white and square. Quite a useful structure, well-kept, and well-loved. The barn is not a landmark. It is not something people travel to glimpse a sight of before it's torn down. Still too functional to be rustic.

This barn is full of hay. There are six cows. Two sheep. And those countless mice which accompany such creatures into the warmth of this place.

It's swept out weekly – less often than it should be but more often than I remember it being 30 years ago when I first entered the red and white doors and climbed up ten bales of hay, through the loft door and onto the waiting fir tree. Higher, higher, higher, until I had a view of town that remains vivid to this day.

In one afternoon, the smell, sight, and sounds of the place managed to transform me from a city kid to a country kid with ease. It wove a magic web of delight around my young body that even Charlotte would be proud of.

It was in that barn I first learned what fear – and courage – are. Where I learned that you could jump down 15 feet from a hayloft into a muddy field and not get injured, although it helped to have a 300-pound cow to land on.

It was in the corner, to the east, where the pigs used to be and morning light danced off steaming cedar, that I learned magnifying glass really does make fire – and courage is admitting that to your parents.

It was in that barn I tried my first glass of homemade wine, and took my first shot with a rifle. In both cases it would be a long time until I ever tried again. But that's the thing about barns. They are places of firsts.

Calves, piglets, and chicks take their first breaths there, see their first sights inside the shelter, take their first tentative steps into an uncertain future. Farmers do their first calving there, kill their first chicken, savour the first hours of sunlight.

We hold onto barns the way we hold onto snapshots of favourite moments from the past – a little too long, until they are worn and ragged. We watch them disintegrate before our eyes and can't quite throw them away.

There are many such memories still standing in Maple Ridge. A tour down the rural end of the busy thoroughfare of Dewdney Trunk Road will prove that. Or a drive through the quiet backstreets of the eastern communities of Ruskin or Whonnock. Fancy new homes may occupy old farmsteads, while aging, unused barns are allowed to fade away with a dignity and distance saved for more cherished places.

Maybe others have learned their own first lessons in these places. Maybe these moss-covered relics remain red, and white, and square in all our minds. Full of cows and pigs. A beebee gun or two. An illicit magnifying glass or sip of wine. Perhaps, those once functional walls are still letting in the morning light through cracks in our memories.

The trees are beautiful
and fun to climb.
There are lots of farms.
My grandparents are here.
There is a creek running
through my back yard.
Jennifer Andreasen, 8

*Local barns, such as the one standing on the well-known Laity
Farm, or this example at Rainforest Gardens on 224th Street,
remain treasured landmarks in Maple Ridge.*

BY OLWYN GEELING

Free range eggs and fresh fruit:
both are still in abundance
in the rural areas of Maple Ridge.

. . . .

Skaters take advantage of the weather

to put one of hundreds of frozen ponds

to good use.

HOCKEY

On the third cold day
they were out early
their skates on the ice
echoing the sound of distant geese

At the far side
it wasn't thick enough
and when the puck slished
to the wet, waving edge
they slid, spread-eagled
and hooked it back

One of them
taller than the rest
lay flat
tapped with a hammer
where the ice held doubt
and, bat like
received reflected sounds
that translated into parts of inches
and a game that would last long enough

Once they had chosen sides
gloved up their goalies
and faced off
they played
as if the ice was ten feet thick

ALAN WOODLAND

I like to play street
hockey in Maple Ridge.
I like to play soccer in
Maple Ridge. I like to play
football in Maple Ridge.
I like to play lacrosse in
Maple Ridge. I like ice
rinks in Maple Ridge.

Kyle Abramyk, 7

BY RON HEDRICK

Back to the Store *BY LYNN EASTON*

Up to the corner store we go with toboggan gliding on knee-deep snow. There's nothing that we need in this blizzard – except the companionship of others.

A quick hello. Eggs, milk, and the news of the day. Familiar faces will share thoughts on when the plough will reach us, rumours of power outages, promises of rain.

There is silence in the snow. It is not 1927, or 1913, or 1902 but it could be, and I indulge the image trudging northward into the past.

The first store for miles was built just ahead, at Webster's Corners, past that remaining farm and across from the now-thriving elementary school. There were no roads then, only rough trails leading from homesteads to this hub of hospitality.

You could collect your mail there, they say. Get news from those back home in Finland, or Mount Fuji, Norway or Niagara. The building was turned into a church once. Services held between the flour and the three-inch hammer nails, I suppose. No dances though. They built a hall for that with parties that went all night. Fiddles on fire, keeping everyone warm.

School, store and hall. Isn't that all you really needed for a town? Every community had them. Hammond mourned as its store was lost in the fire of 1916. Ruskin lamented a similar loss just a few years ago: places of community, somewhere to play a game of cards or talk about the new folks in town. They were a warm welcome on a stormy winter afternoon.

Just like today – nowhere to go but the corner store. It is warm. The lights and coffee are on. The past will fade with the snow-covered footprints behind me. Perhaps. "Hello," I say, warming quickly. "Eggs. Milk. And when is the plough coming?..."

While falling, each snowflake scintillates in the
moonlight and shouts, 'I'm unique', out to the
billions of lacy, light angels soaring in the sky.
Stephen Raskewicz, 10

Cashiers and other employees are very friendly,

and passers-by say helpful things like

"Excuse me, you dropped a quarter."

Ross Saare, age 10

. . . .
*Whonnock Feed and Hardware store was an important
local meeting place, and source of both nails and
news for decades on 272nd street.*
BY ROBERTA COMBS

Fresh cut tulips brighten an aging bicycle.

The Billy Miner Pub is located in the historic former
Bank of Montreal building, constructed in the early
1900s as part of the thriving commercial centre of
Port Haney. BY SUZANNE AMENDOLAGINE

OLD PORT HANEY

Weeds now cover foundations
Of stores, hotels and blacksmith shops,
Only the old bank, converted
Gives any sense of the past.

Haney Station had the prettiest garden,
It's left to the mind's eye to see.
The train doesn't stop here now,
Just hurries by, poignantly.

There's strength in the powerful river,
Yet it embraces the wharf and float.
It speaks of a distant memory of steamers and river boats.

We can still visit Port Haney's founders
Whose names were Thomas and Ann
Their portraits cover the walls
Of a charming house, that still stands.

There's very little remaining,
Of our local history.
Proud towns cherish their past
For future generations to see.

ALANNAH PREST

. . . .

*Taking in the scenery, on Dewdney
Trunk Road just east of 232nd Street
where a field of brilliant yellow
buttercups attracts admirers each spring.*

Horsies.

I see horsies.

Lots of horsies.

Erika Zubek-Nizol, nearly 3

BY RON HEDRICK

Secret Gardens *BY LYNN EASTON*

Hidden off a busy road – a rosebush flourishes.

Apple and plum blossoms throw colour on an open field where blossoms don't belong, offering the promise of sweet fruit from some unknown host. Who had such faith to fill the future with flowers, to put down such strong roots?

These now-quiet cultivators have left us a trail back. They've sent secret gardens to the future for us to find hidden in our neighbour's backyards, between schoolgrounds, on the bright hills of afternoon drives.

A flash of English garden-green lines a single unclaimed splash of Dewdney Trunk Road. No one tends this child of the empire gone wild in the colonies. She is ours now, a gift from the past whose owners have long left.

Wild Whonnock strawberries linger where once a thriving business fed a family. Farmers from the edges of other worlds fled famine, flood, and fear to tear up the earth in this rainforest and start again. Learning the language of this wet place until they spoke with the eloquence of a pink-flowered field ripe sweet with berries.

Greenhouses, the not-so-hidden legacies full of foreign fruits and vegetables, now dot land with efficiency where those red-stained fingers first made space for them.

Untamed rhododendrons wash green and leafy between the cottonwoods and firs in forgotten neighbourhoods from Hammond to Albion.

Seeds of hope have sowed these fruits and flowers where ferns once grew. With optimism to admire, those gardeners worked this westcoast wetland until it produced for them – and us.

As we gather up their wild apples and pluck the last rose we are lucky there are some who still know the recipe for stinging nettle tea and when to gather basil and thyme.

They meet in backyard gardens and over cups of chamomile. They'll turn over the earth again for those who will come looking for strong limbs and wild roses – hidden in the future for hungry hearts to find.

I love the colourful flowers that Mrs. and Mr. Burlington grow. They grow a different kind every spring, and I could never figure out how they got their grass so green. *Keith Jarret, 10*

Mrs. Heather Laity, and one of her many animals, are dwarfed by her gigantic Russian Sunflowers on her family's 128th Avenue farmstead.

· · · · · · · · · · ·

There are still places in Maple Ridge where a young girl

can wile away the hours making daisy chains.

BY ROBERTA COMBS.

A cat is camouflaged amongst a burst of purple asters.

PEAS AND PEONIES

When the moon is right
and the frost has lost its bite
we plant hope in the earth.

Dig in our heels and our spades.
Announce we will stay until the harvest
when the berries have been boiled blood red,
the peaches picked thin. Peas and peonies brought in.

We choose the colours of tomorrow
in the cold kitchens of winter.
Coax shy lavender onto our tables and pillows.
Watch as the land springs alive.
Smile as the willows age
with our earth-stained hands.

LYNN EASTON

Maple Ridge is the place to live,
I think on this drippy morning.
No war, just the sound of
crystal clear water and the
rippling noise of the wind
blowing against the trees.

Pamela Hutchins, 10

*The mist greets an early morning sunrise on
the dykes in west Maple Ridge.*

Simply Sacred BY LYNN EASTON

The Wedding Tree invites.

There is much work that should be done instead. Grocery lists and things-to-do fall from pockets but are stashed back in unseen. Instead, a pair of gloves is retrieved. A blessing as the winter air slides off the Golden Ears in a reminder that spring will come when those glorious beasts are ready to send her – and not a moment before. Thoughts of turning back to a warm car begin to fade as does the chill. Walking. Walking. Walking to the Wedding Tree. This particular dyke, one of countless in this oft-blessed place, has long ago become a church.

That realization came before the Wedding Tree. A child walking alone – when alone was okay – learned that the sporadic sounds of birds and the whipping of wind could conjure up a sense of peace found nowhere else. She learned that the sight of the Golden Ears could humble without a sound.

The endless misty mountains of the northern skyline have indeed been sacred ground to the Katzie people for thousands of years, she learned later. Of course it has she thought, and smiled.

And now this dyke, which looks out to that ancient shrine, is her sacred place. Years of walking here have made it so. Forget the path worn thin with popularity by humans and horses. Forget the line of cars that bring more and more admirers to the unseen doors of this chapel. Forget the cows. Forget the dogs.

There were times she walked here with her own dog along this path. She misses that and thinks of this place as a memorial spot. Plenty of flowers. Golden Ears for the tombstone. Dogs. Dykes. The canines are our excuse to commune with nature. A reason to return.

But she doesn't need an excuse today. Today, she is walking to the Wedding Tree. And here she will sit and smile, listen to the staccato sparrows, shiver in the early spring waiting for whatever message might be on the whipping wind.

The tree doesn't belong to her any more. She is only visiting. It became her children's the minute she told them the story.

The story remains hers. It is enough that her children know this place as nothing else – except the Wedding Tree. They don't think of the irrigation ditch that has just been built across the path. They don't see the endless stream of people. They don't hear the traffic in the distance.

They only see the Wedding Tree and know that this is a sacred spot. Not for a whole people, but for a small family. Not for thousands of years to come, but for awhile yet. Until they find their own spot where a child can walk alone – well, almost alone – and learn to find their own peace in the sounds of the wind.

One night my father opened my
window. He said 'listen to the frogs,
they'll sing you to sleep.'
I like the frogs so much now,
I open my window every night.
Lauren Mallo, 8

A stand of Maples evokes the sense of antiquity

found in our unique landscape.

PLACES IN TIME

The list of Maple Ridge's natural treasures is long: Golden Ears, Gold Creek, Alouette Lake, Kanaka Creek, Whonnock Lake. These sites draw people from halfway across town, the province and the world to this community of more than 60,000 people nestled in the mountains 40 kilometres east of Vancouver, Canada. These are the sites which humble us. Inspire awe in us. Remind us of our history and place. We can't mould them or change them. But they can change us.

A walk through the UBC Malcolm Knapp Research Forest or a hike by an unnamed salmon spawning stream illuminates the special place the natural world plays in our community. The well-known and unknown natural wonders of Maple Ridge are there for all of us to explore. We can still walk out our front doors and be assured of an outdoors experience just minutes away. Through foresight and fortuitous natural design this community can boast trails, hikes, and water systems that astound and attract visitors and residents alike.

The river to the south has given us livelihoods and food, the mountains to the north our weather and wildlife. We in the middle are free to explore, preserve, and ensure our wild spaces flourish. We have been handed a treasure from those who came before and an opportunity to continue their legacy.

MAGIC MOUNTAINS

There's a shell game happening in the sky.

Mountains come and go like hucksters. Tempting us. Tantalizing.
Inviting.

Some say these beings are made of stone. Rock. Unmoved for
millions of years.

But a change in the position of the sun, the shade of a certain
cloud, the angle of a snowfall, and they appear from nowhere.
Mountains that have never stood beside the Golden Ears arise
phoenix-like from the ashes of a winter day to sparkle with a glow
that overshadows these giants.

It happens – watch. Wait.

Why do the Ears, so etched in our minds as a single image of
grandeur and grace, manage to change their own facade so easily
and often? A coat of white some warm May afternoon. Bare and
stark some winter day when they should be tucked up warm in a
blanket of white.

Such questions are for those unaccustomed to the ways of magic.

Pick a mountain. Any mountain. Enjoy the show.

LYNN EASTON

The Golden Ears, which dominate the northern skyline, are part of the coastal mountain range. A strenuous 12-kilometre, seven-hour hike up the Golden Ears trail will provide the gift of a breathtaking view of the Fraser Valley from the 1500-metre summit.

The End of the Road

BY CHRIS CAMPBELL

When we think of 224th Street, does it have just one face?

Images of busy sidewalks and urban traffic are the view most of us see of this downtown thoroughfare. But if you head north towards the mountains, past the frantic pulse of the thriving downtown, you'll find a new perspective here – at the end of the road.

The scenery begins to change as my mountain bike picks up speed. The apartment buildings and offices disappear and the smell of a horse is in the air. The yards gradually grow from postage stamps to acreage size. White picket fences turn to wire to keep horses and cattle in. Group mailboxes used by an entire block morph into a long row of rusting, weather-beaten metal boxes, each emblazoned with a hand-scrawled address and placed on top of a crooked piece of old wood.

One farmer has set up a museum of sorts just inside a fence. It includes six pieces of rusted antique farm equipment, all laid out in a perfect row. Just for good measure, a lone horse wanders this field, munching grass, a reminder of exactly what powered these pieces of equipment before the tractor.

Car traffic has started to dwindle, but the perfect imprint of a horseshoe in the gravel at the side of the road reminds me I have to watch for other things. At the North Alouette River bridge the water level is low. I recall times I've seen this river, controlled not by dams but by nature itself, rise over its banks. For better or for worse, it's an annual reminder that we aren't always in charge of this planet.

I travel past assorted small farms filled with cats, dogs, chickens and one rooster that doesn't realize it isn't dawn. After a few minutes, traffic dies completely. Looking ahead I can sense something. The end is near. For once, that's a good thing. As the end of the road approaches, the animals get a little more exotic. Tiny frogs hop around on green lily pads, each adorned with a single yellow flower. Hundreds of these green and yellow lily pads line a deep ditch filled with water drained from the fields next door.

I'm startled by a Great Blue Heron, equally startled by me, which decides to leave its perch and give a close-up view of its awesome wingspan. By this time, the road has turned from bumpy concrete to even bumpier gravel. The homes have disappeared leaving nothing but mountains, expansive fields and a whole lot of sky.

A street sign, of a kind I've never seen before, tells me the speed limit has plummeted to 10 kilometres an hour. Even I could exceed that, let alone any motor vehicle. This place is strict. Actually, the speed limit is for the bridge over Blaney Creek, a quiet water system that's barely deep enough for a canoe.

In just a few minutes of riding, urban noise has turned into silence, fumes into fresh air, concrete into walking trails. The best part is, the same discovery can be made at most other major roads in Maple Ridge. The northern end of 232nd Street leads all the way to the UBC Malcolm Knapp Research Forest, a treasure trove of spiralling trails. Busy 216th Street ends on a gravel road where you can park and embark on a lengthy dyke trail.

Instead of walking along these trails, I simply sit and watch the Golden Ears in the distance. In a wide span of blue sky, a lone cloud speeds along in the gusts of wind, leaving a shadow on the side of the mountains. That cloud better slow down, I think to myself. In this area, it's liable to get caught for speeding.

*Just minutes out of town quiet streets
and rivers beckon.* BY OLWYN GEELING

I love the way the wind whistles through the trees on a chilly spring day, the way the birds flutter their wings as they fly away because something came near, the way the stream water sparkles from the early morning sunshine. *Jamie Halun*

Striking it Rich at Gold Creek

· · · · · · · · · · · · · · · · · ·

BY CHRIS CAMPBELL

The sun is shining high above, but you can't see it.

This is a dark and lonely stretch of trail that shadows the icy beauty of Gold Creek in Golden Ears Provincial Park. The trees have grown so close together that branches have woven into a leaf and needle tapestry that shields the rays of light.

Somewhere, however, high above, a little hole opens up and a shard of light seizes the opportunity to bolt for the ground. It shines a spotlight on a decapitated tree standing alone three metres off the Lower Falls Trail. Steam rises from this fungus-covered stump as light turns up the furnace to thaw it out.

Light is also shed on a spider's web and the single occupant is not thrilled to be in the spotlight. The spider's many legs traverse the middle of the web in a quest for shade. It's unsuccessful.

Whether or not anyone ever found gold in Gold Creek is unknown, but a few nuggets like this one are easy to discover along the way.

Gold Creek is just the final cache of riches on a 12-kilometre drive through Golden Ears Park. Driving the road is like travelling down a tree-lined hallway, as tall trees form a solid wall of greenery. This hallway has many doors to choose from, but you can't miss no matter which knob you turn. One door takes you to tiny Mike Lake. Another takes you on a day-long journey up the Golden Ears. The most widely used door is to what is essentially the park's living room, the massive Alouette Lake.

Tens of thousands of visitors make the pilgrimage each year to camp out under the stars at Maple Ridge's largest lake, which forms the entire southeastern rim of the park. A series of tributaries, from the smallest streams to the roaring Gold Creek, empty into Alouette Lake. The water then assembles for a busy sojourn as the water gives itself up for use by swimmers, fishers and boaters. Continuing its unselfishness, the lake then gives life to other water systems. An underground pipe supplies water to Stave Lake at one end. A dam seeps water into the South Alouette River, which cuts a path through most of

· ·

The Lower Falls at Gold Creek during a rare summer day
when the water is not thundering quite as loudly as usual.

Maple Ridge before ending up in the Pitt River, Fraser River, and finally the Pacific Ocean. It's amazing to think of the journey one drop of melted snow can take.

One of the best things about Alouette Lake is that it appears to be split in two halves. If you stand on the beach at the day-use area and look past the ridge of mountains on either side, you'll see that the lake narrows, cutting off your view. This creates a sense of mystery, inviting you to canoe past to see what's on the other side. Here, there is a series of campsites only accessible by boat. To enjoy the stunning vistas of the second half of the lake, you'll have to work for it.

Gold Creek is the final door along the hallway. The creek is wide and water is speeding as if each drop is in a hurry for a date with the part of Alouette Lake it empties into. The Lower Falls trail is a 2.7 kilometre journey to a 10-metre high waterfall. With the thunder of the creek to guide the way, the journey heads down the dark trail. Moss is everywhere. On every rock. On every stump. On every branch it hangs like Christmas tinsel.

Eventually, the darkness turns to light at periodic clearings. The first such clearing provides a startling glimpse of the back end of a sharp mountain peak shaped like a head. Mounds of snow fleck its shoulders like dandruff. About halfway up the trail, the noise of Gold Creek turns silent as water pools at a curve in the creek. Here, the water is deep and slow enough to swim in. But it's cold – arctic to be exact. If anyone ever did pan for gold here, they left a few frostbitten fingers. Mountain snow has, however, created water as green as emeralds – another jewel to find.

The trail is mostly flat, requiring little exertion. It allows a casual freedom to think about life, work and the future as you edge along the river. Near the finish, the path abruptly becomes vertical, following the noise of the waterfall. Then you see it.

A wooden observation deck brings people close as the liquid rush comes straight on – so close that mist from the crashing water soaks clothing, and cools hot foreheads. Light streams through trees, forming small rainbows in the falling mist. If you speak, you'll have to yell above the din of the waterfall. But there will be no need for words. You'll simply realize that like those rainbows in the falling mist, you've found gold at the end of the trail.

. . . .

We have come to swim.
Be swallowed up
by this cold mountain gift
of fish, and simple joy.

There is a most appealing rocky trail
just behind me and to the right.
We had some notion
of a climb to an abandoned
logging site – but not today.

Trees four-metres round
were felled by those with brogues
and thick moustaches
Donkeys, railroads, and rough trails
were used to clear this view.

But I won't search them out today.
I believe I'll stay beside this beach
within arms reach of lemonade and
suntan lotion. I am too busy
turning somersaults
in the waves.

LYNN EASTON

BY RONA WILKMAN

I saw a deer run in the forest next to my
house. There is no school today, so our family
is going to the beautiful Alouette Lake.
This is why I love Maple Ridge.
Elizabeth George, 10

Soaking up the sun and tranquillity on Gold Creek,

just minutes away from the

thriving downtown centre of Maple Ridge.

Silence as the sunrises over Alouette Lake

ENCHANTE ALOUETTE

We have come
on a lark
to hear this lake
sing its foreign song,
drip colour on the score,
fill the air with silent wings.

Long sounds of light bounce
off granite hills in some ancient tongue.
Earthbound,
we are still – and moved.
Enchante Alouette

LYNN EASTON

LETTER TO A FRIEND

If you come
come now in May
with the last of the snow on the mountains
and the rhododendrons in bloom

I know you will say
ours are not the wild rhododendrons
that rampage among the hills
in Kashmir, China and Tibet —
and you will be right
But they smoulder and explode
in city parks and gardens
startle out of small neighbourhood yards
and cluster in suspense about the river
an astonishment for the eye
with their variety
of shape and shade

If you come
come now
or lose for a year
or forever
their bold shyness
their courtly beauty
their elegant company

In dappled shade with the snow behind them
you will not miss Kashmir, Tibet, or China
I promise you
Come now

ALAN WOODLAND

Rhododendrons peak through evergreens
at Whonnock Lake.

The Sound of Thunder

. . . .

BY CHRIS CAMPBELL

Kanaka Creek isn't just about visuals.

Breathtaking vistas abound in a spectacular array of trees, creeks, rocks, plant life and animals, all rolled up into one giant sensory explosion. But it's the sound that vibrates my inner core. The roar is faint at first, like an unseen jumbo jet behind the clouds you know is there because it shakes your insides ever so slightly.

Searching for Cliff Falls along Kanaka Creek, I've taken the wrong turn down the North Fork Loop Trail. There are stumps with fungus frisbees jammed into their sides. Tree branches drape over the trail like tines on an umbrella, and sheets of moss cover everything in sight. My only tipoff is the rumble in the distance. The rumble is what I follow.

With each few metres, the rumble turns into a roar that builds. Show time at Cliff Falls, and what a show it is. The sound reaches its epicentre as the water goes through a complicated journey to the creek bottom. The falls drop onto three tiers, each creating a unique sound as the water hits the grey, smooth surfaces, combining into one enormous roar in the observation area above near the edge of a cliff. This is a delightfully noisy place.

It's the most famous part of Kanaka Creek, but by no means the only spectacular audio experience. The Kanaka spirals its way through the southern half of Maple Ridge, with numerous memorable stops along the way. Some areas, like Cliff Falls and the Bell-Irving Hatchery on 256th Street, are easy to find and public. You have to dig a little to find other spots.

Kanaka winds its way down towards the Fraser River through a series of hairpin curves that would make any race car driver dizzy. The creek eventually straightens out at the Kanaka Creek Riverfront Park into an estuary which meets the Fraser.
The search for a lesser-known section of Kanaka continues along a stretch of 112th Avenue. No sign marks the trail, just a steep slope. The trail is well-worn, but raw. Thick tree branches keep out any rays of light. I hear the creek, to my left and 12 metres down, although I'm well above it walking into the unknown.

Thick roots from octogenarian trees bulge out of the ground to provide both excellent footing and treacherous obstacles. The path narrows with hillside to the right and a steep drop-off to the left. Eventually, as the sound of the creek rises again there's a well-used clearing frequented by fishermen whether they are allowed to or not. A deep pool has formed. The three-metre black cliff looks like the hull of an old, battered freighter. Each green plant has five or six fingers that curve up like an outstretched hand. I'm too far away to give 'em five.

Here another waterfall, not quite as big as Cliff Falls but just as loud, is feeding the deep pool. Water crashes down from one level onto the rocks below, only this time the water is coming straight at me. I stand for a few minutes taking in all this sound and fury until it starts to rain. Just a few drops at first, then harder. Soon the footprints on the ground around me will disappear until the next explorer comes along. I know I'm not the first person to discover this place, it just feels that way.

I love Maple Ridge because of
the tall, tall trees; the beautiful
waterfalls and walking trails;
and the way the flowers bloom.
Ashley Armstrong, 9

BY KATHY NAY

There really is no beginning or end to this
creek, no matter what the maps say.
Those trails indeed do belong to the elusive
unicorn. There really are fairies in the moss.

*The water of Kanaka Creek shows its power
as it rushes towards Cliff Falls.*

Paddle.

The rhythm is contagious. Easy – even for arms grown tired from too much time working computer keys and holding steering wheels. Muscles never thought to be tight loosen with every lunge forward.

The sun begins the day with us. Rising with the paddles. Each stroke invokes the morning spirits. They are kind today and bring unexpected warmth while awakening waterdwellers in the mist.

Paddle.

It is too soon to speak. This lake is loud with life and our voices are in the wrong key. The time to sing will come when the noon day sun is high above the wooded shores – after these creatures have had their say. Exhausted, they'll sleep in the reeds, allow us to linger in their home.

Until then – paddle.

In this worn-hulled boat we slip silent into the afternoon. The sun nests in the tops of trees while our paddles slice through grass and this glassy plain, shatter nothing but the silence with our sighs.

This beat-up boat bought with money meant for more practical things – washing machines or mortgages. There was no choice in this decision, though. Borrowed floors and dirty clothes are worth this view. On this lake. This canoe the only way in.

Paddle.

LYNN EASTON

Enjoying the serenity of an early morning paddle on Alouette River.

THE GOLDEN EARS OF TIME

Could it be that ancient Kwant'stan, has kept guard on this place,

Before man stood on two legs, and became a hairless human race,

Before we saw our likeness, upon the full silvery moon,

Before the biblical days of yore, before the forty day monsoon.

Did you see to the west, the masts of George Vancouver's ship,

Or hear the cheers from Greenwich, as he started that long trip,

And see us start to build, the outpost at Fort Langley

And feel us dig your gold, to take back across the sea.

How many times have you watched, and seen the Fraser burst its banks,

At harvest time heard the farmer, look towards you and give thanks,

And heard our new-born cry, and watch them start to grow,

And heard us pray for showers, or curse the drifting snow.

Without asking we changed your name, to the peaks of the 'Golden Ears'

Few are left to call you Kwant'stan, and fewer still with passing years,

But you'll always be there, filling creeks and streams with water,

To feed us all below, Father, Mother, Son and Daughter.

BY ALBERT RICHARD HOOPER

In the Coast Salish, or Halkomelem tongue,
the Golden Ears mountains are referred
to as Kwant'stan.

The majestic rock formation known today as
the Golden Ears has looked down on this
community for all of its 125 years and for
thousands of years before.

. . . . Maple Ridge *Moments in Time* . . . . .

Wild foxgloves line the roadsides throughout Maple Ridge.

BY MARGARET BALE

Herb O Grace A Sun Days

My Catnip
In the tall grass, in feather light beds
perfumed by Lavender
This nose of mine, alive and led from scent to scent
Heady Lemon Balm, Bergamot, my Bee Balm.
Evening Primrose and St. John's Wort to chase away
the blues.
Salve O'Calendula, Comfrey to mend my bones.
Colding away Echinacea, sooth my throat Sage,
Bring me your wisdom.

Weave me a garland
Braided with Pansies, wild Daisies and cream Buttercups.
So as not to Rue the day,
Respect and homage to Belladonna
and heartfelt Foxglove
and the sting of Nettle.

Pour me a cup of Peppermint Tea
Flavour my meal with Basil and Thyme
Borage give me courage
Rosemary helps me to remember
My catnip for a catnap
and a Cheshire smile.

Louise Stephen

The Artists

SUZANNE AMENDOLAGINE is a self-taught visual artist who works in pastel, watercolour acrylic, and now ceramics. Art has remained a constant in her life while she has pursued a variety of careers, lived in locations from Newfoundland to the United States and raised five boys.

MARGARET BALE is a self-taught Maple Ridge watercolour painter who is also exploring the use of collage in her work. Bale has taken part in exhibitions throughout the Fraser Valley and Lower Mainland.

ROBERTA COMBS is an artist who works primarily with watercolour. She has travelled extensively in the U.S. and in the unspoiled regions of B.C. looking for inspiration for her paintings. Combs work can be seen in galleries throughout B.C. and in private collections. She lives in Pitt Meadows with her husband Lee and her two children.

OLWYN GEELING is an artist who works from her Maple Ridge studio. Her internationally known collections can be found in France, Belgium, Holland, England, Canada, and the United States. She is also a local art instructor and demonstrator.

RON HEDRICK is an oil painter who also experiments in a variety of other mediums. He has recently been voted in as a member of an international network of the Salmagundi Club on New York's Fifth Avenue. His work is on display at galleries across Canada and the United States.

CINDI HOFLIN is a 30-year resident of Maple Ridge. She works in a variety of mediums but her passion remains oil painting.

KATHY NAY is a watercolour artist and longtime resident of Maple Ridge. She was the 1998-99 president of the Garibaldi Art Club and is an active member of the Canadian Federation of Artists. Her work has recently hung in the CFA's gallery on Granville Island.

MARILYN TIMMS is a former long-time Maple Ridge watercolour painter who now resides in Courtney, B.C. She was a featured artist at the Espace Culturel Paul Ricard Ile de Bendor, in France in 1996. Timms has also taken part in juried competitions in Australia, the U.S. and Canada.

RONA WILKMAN is a painter who works mainly in oil paints from her home studio in Maple Ridge. She is a member of the Canadian Federation of Artists and has shown in group exhibitions at Granville Island. She has also displayed her work at Britannia Beach Gallery, Maple Ridge Art Gallery, and Place des Arts in Port Moody.

ELWOOD HEWGILL began exploring the medium of watercolour painting when he retired in 1980, after years of travelling BC. He was born in Clarksburg, Ontario in 1915 where his love of landscape developed. Hewgill is a well-respected member of the Maple Ridge arts community.

Ridge Meadows Community Arts Council

The arts and cultural life in Maple Ridge has been enriched through the leadership provided by the Ridge Meadows Arts Council for almost three decades. Known originally as the T'Lagunna Fine Arts Council, then the Maple Ridge Arts Council, the present day Ridge Meadows Community Arts Council has been supporting and promoting arts and culture in the communities of Maple Ridge and Pitt Meadows since 1971.

As a registered non-profit charity, the Arts Council serves as an umbrella organization for artists, arts groups, arts supporters and citizens.

The Arts Council strives to advance arts and culture through arts education, special events like the annual Family Arts Fair, the Voice of the Arts newsletter, scholarship programmes, Poetry in the Gallery, and co-sponsored activities such as art exhibitions at the Maple Ridge Art Gallery. The Arts Council's vision for the future focuses on a longtime dream of building a multi-disciplinary arts centre in the heart of Maple Ridge.

The Arts Council draws its strength from the partnerships it has developed particularly with the Ridge Meadows Parks and Leisure Services Commission. A strong foundation has been built, but it will take strong, committed visionaries to carry it into the future.

Maple Ridge Historical Society

Ever since 1956, the Maple Ridge Historical Society has been promoting and protecting the heritage of Maple Ridge. Through public events and programs, they have explored and publicized our unique history, as the fifth community in British Columbia to seek incorporation back in 1874. Now the Maple Ridge Historical Society oversees operation of the1888 brick St. Andrew's Presbyterian Church in Port Haney, restored and used as a meeting place. The Society has also preserved and restored the Old Post Office on Calligan Street, now operating as a preschool.

The Maple Ridge Museum, in the Haney Brick and Tile Company building, is another major project of the Maple Ridge Historical Society. Year-round tours and educational projects are held at the museum using the collected artifacts and archives that have been preserved in the District of Maple Ridge. The Society also oversees the operation of Haney House, donated to the District, in 1976. The Society is active in many forms of heritage, including the annual summer Music on the Wharf concert series, bringing people and celebrations to the restored Port Haney Wharf. Displays in the community help the Society keep our heritage before the public, and build support for preservation of valued historical landmarks.